Elizabeth Porter Gould

Stray Pebbles From the Shores of Thought

Elizabeth Porter Gould

Stray Pebbles From the Shores of Thought

ISBN/EAN: 9783744651882

Printed in Europe, USA, Canada, Australia, Japan

Cover: Foto ©Thomas Meinert / pixelio.de

More available books at **www.hansebooks.com**

STRAY PEBBLES

FROM THE

SHORES OF THOUGHT

BY

ELIZABETH PORTER GOULD

BOSTON
PRESS OF T. O. METCALF & CO.
1892

CONTENTS.

iii

Poems of Love:

Presence.

CONTENTS.   v

POEMS OF NATURE.

TO WALT WHITMAN.

"I loafe and invite my soul."
And what do I feel?
An influx of life from the great central
    power
That generates beauty from seedling to
    flower.

"I loafe and invite my soul."
And what do I hear?
Original harmonies piercing the din
Of measureless tragedy, sorrow, and sin.

"I loafe and invite my soul."
And what do I see?
The temple of God in the perfected man
Revealing the wisdom and end of earth's
    plan.

August, 1891.

11

TO SUMMER HOURS.

DAY.

Trip lightly, joyous hours,
While Day her heart reveals.
Such wealth from secret bowers
King Time himself ne'er steals.
O joy, King Time ne'er steals !

NIGHT.

Breathe gently, tireless hours,
While Night in beauty sleeps.
Hold back e'en softest showers,—
Enough that mortal weeps.
Ah me, that my heart weeps !

A TRUE VACATION.

IN A HAMMOCK.

"Cradled thus and wind caressed,"
Under the trees,
(Oh what ease.)
Nature full of joyous greeting;
Dancing, singing, naught secreting,
Ever glorious thoughts repeating —
Pause, O Time,
I'm satisfied!
Now all life
Is glorified!

Porter Manse, Wenham, Mass.

13

A QUESTION.

Is life a farce?
Tell me, O breeze,
Bearing the perfume of flowers and trees,
While gaily decked birds
Pour forth their gladness in songs beyond
    words,
And cloudlets coquette in the fresh summer
    air
Rejoicing in everything being so fair —
Is life a farce?

How can it be, child,
When Nature at heart
Is but the great spirit of love and of art
Eternally saying, " I must God impart."

Is life a farce?
Tell me, O soul,
Struggling to act out humanity's whole
'Midst Error and Wrong,
And failure in sight of true victory's song;
With Wisdom and Virtue at times lost to
view,
And love for the many lost in love for the
few —
Is life a farce?

How can it be, child,
When humanity's heart
Is but the great spirit of love and of art
Eternally crying, " I must God impart."

TO A BUTTERFLY.

O butterfly, now prancing
    Through the air.
    So glad to share
The freedom of new living,
Come, tell me my heart's seeking.
    Shall I too know
    After earth's throe
Full freedom of my being?
    Shall I, as you,
    Through law as true,
Know life of fuller meaning?

O happy creature, dancing,
    Is time too short
    With pleasure fraught
For you to heed my seeking?

Ah, well, you've left me thinking :
  If here on earth
  A second birth
Can so transform a being,
  Why may not I
  In worlds on high
Be changed beyond earth's dreaming ?

IN A HAMMOCK.

The rustling leaves above me,
The breezes sighing round me,
A network glimpse of bluest sky
To meet the upturned seeing eye,
The greenest lawn beneath me,
Loved flowers and birds to greet me,
A well-kept house of ancient days
To tell of human nature's ways,—
    Oh happy, happy hour!

Whence comes all this to bless me,
The soft wind to caress me,
The life which does my strength renew
For purer visions of the true?
Alas! no one can tell me.

But, hush ! let Nature lead me.
Let even wisest questions cease
While I breathe in such life and peace
This happy, happy hour.

Porter Manse, Wenham, Mass.

O RARE, SWEET SUMMER DAY.

"The day is placid in its going,
    To a lingering motion bound,
Like a river in its flowing —
    Can there be a softer sound?"
                — *Wordsworth*.

O rare, sweet summer day,
    Could'st thou not longer stay?
The soothing, whispering wind's caress
    Was bliss to weary brain,
The songs of birds had power to bless
    As in fair childhood's reign.

The tinted clouds were free from showers,
    The sky was wondrous clear,
The precious incense of rare flowers
    Made sweet the atmosphere;

20

The shimmering haze of mid-day hour
Was balm to restlessness,
While thought of silent hidden power
Was strength for helplessness —
O rare, sweet summer day,
Could'st thou not longer stay?

Porter Manse.

AN OLD MAN'S REVERIE.

Blow breezes, fresh breezes, on Love's
    swiftest wing,
And bear her the message my heart dares
    to sing.
Pause not on the highways where gathers
    earth's dust,
Nor in the fair heavens, though cloudlets
    say must.
But blow through the valleys where flowers
    await
To give of their essence ere yielding to
    fate ;
Or blow on the hill tops where atmospheres
    lie
Imbued with the health which no money
    can buy.

But fail not, O breezes, on Love's swiftest
    wing
To bear her the message my heart dares to
    sing.

The breezes, thus ladened, sped on in their
    flight,
As, cradled in hammock, I sang in delight,
On that blest summer day in the years long
    ago,
When life was all sunshine and youth all
    aglow.
The sweets of the valleys, the breath of the
    hills
Were gathered — the best that our loved
    earth distills —
As, ·obedient still to my wish, on they flew
To the home of my darling they now so
    well knew.

*   *   *   *   *   *

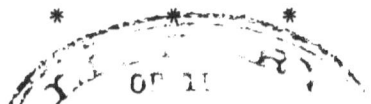

Alas for the breezes, alas for my heart,
Alas for my message, so full of love's art !
If only the breezes had followed their will,
And loitered among the pure cloudlets so
 still,
They'd have met a fair soul from the earth
 just set free
In search of their help for its message to
 me ;
The message my darling, with last fleeting
 breath,
In vain tried to utter, o'ertaken by death.

The breezes, fresh breezes, have blown on
 since then,
With messages laden again and again.
As for me, I send none. I wait only their
 will
To bring me that message my lone heart
 to fill.

They'll find it some day in a light zephyr
  chase,
For nothing is lost in pure love's boundless
  space.

ON JEFFERSON HILL.

(BEFORE THE PRESIDENTIAL RANGE.)

The sovereign mountains bask in sunset
rays,
The valleys rest in peace;
The lingering clouds melt into twilight haze,
The birds their warbling cease;
The villagers' hour of welcome sleep is
near,
The cattle wander home,
While wrapped in summer-scented atmos-
phere,
Calm evening comes to roam
With gentle pace
Through star-lit space,

26

Till moon-kissed Night holds all in her
embrace,
And Morning waits to show her dawn-
flushed face.

ON SUGAR HILL.

TO F. B. F.

The lovely valleys nestling in the arms
  Of glorious mountain peaks ;
The purple tint of sunset hour, and charms
  The evening hour bespeaks ;
The monarch peak kissed by the rising sun,
  While clouds keep guard below ;
Grand, restful views, with foliage autumn-
  won,
  And Northern lights rare glow,—
    Will e'er recall,
    In memory's hall,
The happy days when on fair " Look-Off's "
  height,
Sweet friendship cast her hues of golden
  light.

Hotel Look-Off, September, 1891.

AT FAIRFIELDS*, WENHAM.

June, 1890.

Buttercups and daisies,
  Clover red and white,
Ferns and crown-topped grasses
  Waving with delight,
Dainty locust-blossoms,
  All that glad June yields,
Welcome me with gladness
  To dearly-loved " Fairfields."
But where's my happy collie dog,
  My Rosa ?

The orioles sing greeting,
  The butterflies come near,

---

* " Fairfields " is but another name for " Porter Manse."

The hens cease not their cackling,
· The horses neigh " I'm here,"
The cows nod " I have missed you,"
The pigs' eyes even shine,
And from the red-house hearth-stone
Comes pet cat Valentine.
But where's my happy collie dog,
My Rosa?

I miss her joyful greeting,
Her handsome, high-bred face,
Her vigorous, playful action
In many a fair field chase.
Not even lively Sancho
Can fill for me her place.

O Rosa, happy Rosa,
Gone where the good dogs go,
Dost find such fields as "Fairfields,"
More love than we could show?

BLOSSOM-TIME.

Blossoms floating through the air,
Bearing perfumes rich and rare,
Free from trouble, toil, and care.
Would I were a blossom !

Robins singing in the trees,
Feeling every velvet breeze,
Free from knowledge that bereaves.
Would I were a robin !

Violets peaceful in the vale,
Telling each its happy tale,
Free from worldly noise and sale.
Would I were a violet !

Blessed day of needed wealth,
Full of Nature's perfect health,
Fill me with thy power.

31

Then like blossoms I shall be,
        Wafting only purity,
Or like robins, singing free
'Midst the deepening mystery,
Or like violets, caring naught
Only to reflect God's thought."

Porter Manse.

THE PRIMROSE.

Who tells you, sweet primrose, 'tis time to
    wake up
    After dreaming all day?
Who changes so quickly your sombre green
    dress
    To the yellow one gay,
And makes you the pet of the twilight's
    caress,
    And of poet's sweet lay?
    Who does, primrose, pray?

The primrose, secure on his emerald throne,
    Looked up quickly to say,
"A dear lovely fairy glides down from his
    throne
    In the sun's golden ray,

33

And with a sweet kiss opens wide all our
          eyes,
     Saying, 'Now is your day.'
And lo! when he's gone we are filled with
          surprise
     At our wondrous array,
     So fresh and so gay.
Do tell us the name of this fairy, I pray,
Who gives of his beauty, and then hies
          away
     Without thanks, without pay.
     Does he linger your way?"

JOY, ALL JOY.

Lying on the new-mown hay, in a sightly
    field,
  On a summer day,
  With no care to weigh,
Or a bitter thought to stay all that sense
    might yield —
  What a joy to have alway!

Sky as blue as blue can be, perfect green
    all round,
  Birdlings on the wing
  Ere they pause to sing
On the top of bush or tree, or on sweet
    hay-mound —
  Restful joy in everything!

Butterflies just come to light, proud of free-
dom's hour,
Cows in pastures near,
Wondering why I'm here,
Chipmunks now and then in sight, bees in
clover-flower —
Added joy when these appear !

Happy children far and near climbing loads
of hay,
Running here and there.
Farmer's work to share,
Skipping, shouting loud and clear, full of
daring play —
Children's joy ! Joy everywhere !

AMONG THE PINES.

Far up in air the pines are murmuring
  Love songs sweet and low,
  With a rhythmic flow,
Worthy of the glad sun's glow.

The airy clouds are o'er them bending,
  Captured by the sound
  Of such pleasure found
In a playful daily round.

The birds pause in their flight to listen,
  Wondering all the while
  How the trees can smile
Rooted so to earthly guile.

37

The hush of summer noon enwraps them
    Perfumed from below
    By the flowers that show
They, too, murmuring love songs know.

All nature finds a joy in loving —
    Oh, that I could hear
    Love songs once so dear
Death has hushed forever here !

Intervale Woods, North Conway.

CONSCIOUS OR UNCONSCIOUS?

The earthquake's shock, the thunder's roar,
   The lightning's vivid chain,
The ocean's strength, the deluge's pour,
   The wildest hurricane,

Are moods that Nature loves to show
   To man who boasts his birth
From conscious force she could not know
   Because denied soul-worth.

But is it true she does not share
   A knowledge in God's plan?
Must not she His own secret bear
   To so touch soul of man?

Those who deny this see not clear
  Into the heart of things;
For how could otherwise God here
  Reveal His wanderings?

POEMS OF LOVE.

The days are restful here, dear,
With thy sweet ministry;
All nature feels the breath of love
And life 'e a symphony.

Eye drinks in all the beauty,
Full heart the music feels,
While over all the hopes and fear
God's benediction steals.

E. P. S.

LOVE'S HOW AND WHY.

How do I love thee?
Oh, who knows
How the blush of the rose
Can its secret disclose?
Oh, who knows?

Why do I love thee?
Ah, who cares
Sound a passion he shares
With the angels? Who dares,
Yes, who dares?

LOVE'S GUERDON.

Thine eyes are stars to hold me
   To love's pure rapturous height.
Thy thoughts are pearls to lead me
   To truth beyond earth's sight.
Thy love is life to keep me
   Forever in God's light.

A BIRTHDAY GREETING.

Thy birthday, dear?
Oh, would I had the poet's art
By which I could my wish impart
    For thy new year;
But e'en a poet's pen of gold
Would fail my wish to thee unfold
    In earthly sphere.

Thy birthday, dear?
Oh, would I had the painter's skill
Prophetic visions to fulfill
    For thy new year;
But e'en a painter's rarest brush
Would but my holy visions crush,
    Or fail to cheer.

45

Thy birthday, dear?
Oh, would I had sweet music's aid
To vitalize the prayers I've made
    For thy new year;
Alas! not even music's best
Could put in form my soul's behest
    For thee, my dear.

That only will expression find
In purest depths of thine own mind
    This coming year;
As, guided by the inner light,
There'll come to thee the new-born sight
    Of ravished seer.

But in this sight thou may'st so feel
Eternal beauty o'er thee steal —
    God's gift, my dear —
That thou can'st find the blessed art

Of making even

~~By which to make~~ e'en depths of heart
In form appear.

Yet, it may be a heaven's birthday
Will have to dawn for us to say
Our best things, dear.
For, as thou know'st, Truth's deepest well
Must e'er reflect, its depths to tell
Heaven's atmosphere.

THREE KISSES.

The kiss still burns upon my brow,
  That kiss of long ago,
When in the flush of love's first hour
  He said he loved me so.

Another burns yet deeper still,
  The kiss of wedded bliss,
When soul met soul in rapture sweet —
  Oh, pure love's burning kiss !

The third was laid away with him,
  A kiss for heaven's day,
  (O heart abide God's way) --
When in the life beyond earth's change,

Beyond these mysteries sad and strange,
New life will spring from out the old,
New thoughts will larger truth unfold,
 And love have endless sway.

IF I WERE ONLY SURE.

If I were only sure
He loves me still,
As in the realms of beauteous space
(Alas! so far from my embrace)
He bides God's will,
I could be more content to bear
The bitter anguish and despair
Which now me fill.

If I were only sure
He waits for me
To join him in the heavenly realm
(Oh, how the thought does overwhelm)
When body-free,

I could the better bear my fate,
As day by day I learn to wait
   In silent agony.

   O Father, in my doubt
   One thing is sure,
That Thou, all love, could ne'er destroy
(Death only is in earth's alloy)
   Such love so pure
As that which blessed our union here,
The love which knew no change nor fear —
   Such must endure.

ABSENCE.

The days are happy here, dear,
But happier would they be
Could'st thou be near to bless me
With love's sweet ministry ;

Then all this beauty round me
Would on my memory lie,
As prayers of sainted mother,
Or childhood's lullaby.

Hotel Look-Off, Sugar Hill, N.H.

52

A LOVE SONG.

Oh ! ecstasy rare
Comes down to share
The heart that with human love trembles ;
While all on the earth
Is crowned with new birth
And everything heaven resembles.

But grief and despair
Have latent their share
In hearts that with human love tremble,
Since fires of love
Enkindled above
In frail earthen vessels assemble.

Still, ecstasy rare
Comes down to share

The heart that with human love trembles;
   While all on the earth
   Is crowned with new birth
And everything heaven resembles.

IN HER GARDEN.

She picks me June roses.
Were ever such roses?
Their fragrance would honor
The heavenly halls.

She finds me pet pansies.
Such wondrous-eyed pansies,
And lovely nasturtiums
That run on the walls.

Sweet peas she's now bringing,
While all the time singing.
And I? Ask the flowers
To tell what befalls.

LOVE'S WISH.

Would I were beautiful !
Then you at Beauty's shrine might freely
dine,
A welcome guest
For joy's bequest.
But, dear, if this were so,—
If I were Beauty's child, all undefiled,
To make you blest
In beauty's quest,

You might forget to see
The soul's pure hidden shrine wherein e'er
shine
The things that test
Love's true behest.

Would I were beautiful,
That you might better see the soul in me!
That wish is best,
Is 't not, dearest?

IS THERE ANYTHING PURER?

Oh, the prayer of a dear virgin-heart,
Breathed forth with true love's gentle art!
    Is there anything purer
      On land or on sea,
    More laden with blessing
      For you or for me?

It is sweeter than song ever heard,
More precious than love's spoken word.
It is fraught with a keen recognition
Of truest soul-need and fruition.
    Is there anything purer
      On land or on sea,
    More laden with comfort
      For you or for me?

It is oftentimes born in great pain,
With no ray of hope's blessed gain.
But as lulled by the angels at midnight
Ere reaching the infinite daylight
    Is there anything surer,
      On land or on sea,
    To bring the God-Father
      To you or to me ?

LONGING.

Through all this summer joy and rest,
Though lying on fair Nature's breast,
There breathes the longing heart's desire,
  Would he were here!

The thrill of pain kind Nature feels;
For all the while there o'er me steals
Like holy chimes in midnight air,
  " He'll soon be here."

And flowers and trees, vales, hills, and birds
Make haste to echo her glad words,
  " He'll soon be here."

YOUNG LOVE'S MESSAGE.

Sing too, little bird, what my heart sings
    to-day.
        Dost thou know? —
        I'll speak low —
    "Oh, I do love him so."

Hold safe, waving grass, in thy rhythmical
    flow,
        What I say,
        Till the day
    When as sweet new-mown hay

Thou can'st bear it to him in the fragrance
    loved best.

Thou dost fear?—
Oh, love dear,
How I wish thou wert here!

But pause, little cloud, thou canst carry it
  now,
      I am sure,
      Sweet and pure,
Though the winds do allure:

For thou art on the way to the west where
  he is.
      But dost know?—
      Tell him low,
" That I do love him so,
Oh! I do love him so."

A DIARY'S SECRET.

January 1, 1867.

God's love was once enough
My heart to satisfy,
When in the days of childhood's faith
I knew not doubt or sigh.

But since I saw Roy's face,
And knew his love's sweet cheer,
And felt the anguish and despair
Which come from partings here,

So hungry have I grown
No love can satisfy,
And all my childhood's faith in God
Doth mock me as a lie.

But still in these dark hours
I hold one anchor fast :
Perhaps this is the *woman's* way
To reach God's love at last.

January 1, 1887.

The deepening years have proved
Love's conquest justified.
The woman's hungry heart at last
In God is satisfied.

A MONOLOGUE.

Has Love come?
Ah, too late!
Already Death stands o'er me
With hungry eyes that bore me —
    O cruel fate,
    That after all life's years
    Of sacrifice and tears,
'Tis Death, not Love, that wins.
But, stay! This message bear,
Ere yet Death's work begins:
" In other realms earth's losses
Will change from saddening crosses
    To love-crowned joy,
Where Death shall have no mission,
But Love his sweet fruition
    Without alloy."

65

A PRICELESS GIFT.

'T was much he asked — a virgin heart
  Unknown to worldly ways.
What could he give? Ah, well he knew
  He lacked sweet virtue's praise.

The virgin heart was given to him
  Without a doubting thought,
When, lo ! through seeming sacrifice
  A miracle was wrought ;

A miracle of love and grace,
  Revealing woman's power ;
For, clothed in purity, he rose
  To meet the coming hour.

THE OCEAN'S MOAN.

Last night the ocean's moan
  Was to my ears
The deep sad undertone
  Of vanished years,

Bearing a burden,
A bliss unattained,
A strife and a longing,
A life sad and pained,
To the shores vast and free
Of eternity's sea.

But in that undertone
  Of restless pain,
Came at length a monotone
  Of sweet refrain,

Bearing a passion
Long known to the sea —
Told in moments of silence
A sad heart to free —
To be borne me some day
In the ocean's own way.

And this rare monotone
    Of mystery
Was now that passion-moan
    Of secrecy,

Bearing, " I love her,
My moaning ne'er'll cease
Till she on my breast
Findeth love's perfect peace ;
Till she on my breast
Findeth love's perfect rest."

Oh, is there tenderer tone
    For mortal ear,

Than such a monotone,
Distinct and clear,

Bearing its comfort,
Its heavenly peace,
Its help for all sorrow,
Its heart-pain release,
To a soul waiting long
For love's tender, true song?

And now the ocean's moan
Is to my ears
The dearest undertone
Of all the years,

Bearing a memory,
A sweet bliss attained,
A gratified longing,
A life's joys regained,
To the shores vast and free
Of eternity's sea.

Boar's Head, Hampton, N.H.

LOVE'S FLOWER.

Love's sweet and tender flower
  Of pure, perennial life,
Blooms ever fresh in power
  O'er all earth's wrong and strife.

Pluck not in haste, young man,
  This flower of wondrous hue,
Nor dare to crush, nor fail to scan,
  Such beauty ever new.

Gaze at it long, young girl,
  And guard its sacred blush;
Then shall its treasures old unfurl
  Your yearning soul to hush.

LOVE DISCROWNED.

SCENE I.

" When he comes, my darling,
  I shall tell him all:
All the secret ecstasy,
  All the peace and joy,
All my heart's sweet fantasy,
  Free from self's alloy,—
All —

  O blessed power
  Of love's sweet hour,
When I shall tell him all,
  Shall tell him all ! "

SCENE II.

" Hark, hark ! he's come.   I hear his step.
  O joy, love's hour is here.
I knew that he was true and pure,
  I could not feel love's fear.
  Oh, no ; I could not, dear."

SCENE III.

She gave one look, one piercing look,
  Drew back her anguished soul,
Then murmured low, "O bitter hour !
  But — God — forgive — the — whole—
Forgive —

      O bitter power
      Of love's death-hour,
  I thought to tell him all,
    To tell him all."

SCENE IV.

He gazed upon her lifeless face,
He held her lifeless hand.
Was this the form he once had loved ?
He did not understand.
Once loved ?   Yes, that was so.
He'd loved since, one or two,
And — well, what was a woman for,
If not for man to woo ?

MORAL.

Alas, for broken hearts and lives
Of those who can but trust !
Alas, for those who see no law
But that of selfish must !

RENUNCIATION.

"Oh, is not love eternal
  When once the heart be won?
Oh, is not love infernal
  When love can be undone?"

So sighed a gentle maiden
  In light of memory dear,
As, sad and heavy-laden,
  She longed for knowledge clear.

But soon the bitter heart-ache
  Gave way to victory's cheer;
For, brave, she chose for His sake
  The life which knows no peer;

The life of abnegation
  Which gives the Christ's own peace,
But leaves the sad temptation
  To ask for life's release.

A WIDOW'S HEART-CRY.

"Thy will, not mine, be done!"
So breathe I when the day's begun,
So breathe I when the day is done.

I whisper it in blinding tears,
I pause and listen, till appears
The welcome voice for listening ears;

The voice which checks my wayward will
And makes my longing heart to thrill
With love for those who need me still.

But, O, how long must I so pray?
When will I learn to calmly say,
"Thy will is mine," both night and day?

Ah! this can never be on earth,
Since he who gladly gave me birth
To everything that was of worth

Has gone from out my sense and sight,
To what? O ye who still invite
To heaven's sure realm and faith's own
   right,

Reveal some clue for me to see
What life is his, what he's to me.
Alas! ye can't. Then what can be

More precious when the day is done,
Or when the morning is begun,
Than, " Not my will, but Thine, be done."

TOGETHER.

Transformed, redeemed from all that dwarfs
  or blights,
In perect harmony with beauteous sights
Beyond imagination's highest flights
    Ere reached by seer,
We shall together walk the golden streets
    Sometime, my dear.

But how, you ask, shall we each other know,
So changed from what we were while here
  below,
When, caged like birds, we longed and suf-
  fered so?
    Ah, do not fear.

78

Will not the soul, when free, seek like the
   bird
      Its own, my dear?

It may not be at once or soon, 'tis true.
For you may be among the blessed few
Who'll sooner reach the blissful heights —
      your due
         For pure life here —
But sometime, sure as God is love and truth,
      We'll meet, my dear.

Some precious, long-forgotten look or word
Breathed through the softest, sweetest music
      heard,
Or some vibration rare of soul depths stirred
      By memory's tear,
Will, like a flash of light, reveal our souls
      Together, dear,
To live the fuller life we've dreamed of here.

SHADOWED CIRCLES.

Why weepest thou, O dear one?
    Do sorrows press?
Beneath the weight of sorrow
    Is love's caress.

Why joyest thou, O dear one?
    Is love thine own?
Ah! 'neath love's deep rejoicing
    Is sorrow's moan.

Indeed, all earth's great passions —
    Is it not so? —
Are circled in the shadow
    Of joy or woe.

But why should we bemoan this?
    Could otherwise
Truth's dazzling light be subject
    To mortal eyes?

Could otherwise we enter
    The endless light,
Beyond the shadowed circle
    Of mortal sight?

And Nature sings through all our earthly wa[ys]
    There is no death;
    All is the breath
Of life that opens to an Easter-day.

And Love sings, too, 'midst all the pain and st[rife]
    There is no death;
    Hear what it saith?
"I am the Resurrection and the Life."

O glorious song of Nature and of Love!
    On, onward ring..
    Till all hearts sing
There is no death, 'tis life from God above.

           E. P. S.

MISCELLANEOUS POEMS.

Why not!
The waves are kissing the shore,
And trees are greeting each other,
The lake is aglow with the love of the su
And rocks feel the kisses of trees they have,
The breezes are sighing,
And mated birds flying
Sweet flowers are opening their hearts to the t
While ivy is kissing the rocks and the tr
Fair clouds are coquetting
In June's bluest sky —
All nature loves petting —
Then why shouldn't I?

A SONG OF SUCCESS.

I am dancing along.   Just to live is a joy,
 I'm so happy and free.
I know not nor care what will tame or de-
 stroy,
 Life now satisfies me.
 Oh, there's naught like dear youth
 To reveal the glad truth
That 'tis pure, healthful joy just to know
 and to be !

MIDDLE AGE.

I am marching along, full of work and of
 plan
 To alleviate wrong.

85

With a heart full of love both to God and
    to man,
And an arm free and strong.
Oh, there's naught like mid-life
To make sure without strife
The beauty of progress through action and
    song.

OLD AGE.

I am living along, sitting down by the way.
    My work is all done.
I have fought the good fight, known the full
    of each day,
    And true victory won.
Oh, there's naught like old age
To declare with the sage,
Life ending on earth is but heaven begun.

THE UNDER-WORLD.

Under the restless surface
Of ocean's vast domain,
The god of perfect quiet
Holds ever peaceful reign.

Under the restless surface
Of passions strong and wild,
The still small voice of conscience
Is heard in accents mild.

Under the restless surface
Of all man's life on earth,
The Christ of sacred story
Renews each day his birth.

SHE KNOWS.

*(Written at Mountain Cottage, on Mount Wachusett, where
Louisa M. Alcott spent the last summer of her life.)*

Last summer she believed that in and
through these beauteous scenes
God's loving self did flow,
But now she knows 'tis so.

For, having crossed the boundary lines of
honest doubt and fear,
She sees with spirit-eye
What sense could not descry.

Her firm belief, thus blossomed into perfect
flower of sight,
Becomes a restful cheer
To all who linger here,

88

Still asking for the secret of these changing,
    beauteous scenes,
    And troubled with the why
    Of all earth's sorrowing cry.

Her presence here has filled the place with
    memory of a soul
    Made beautiful through pain
    Eternity to gain.

August, 1888.

AT PITTSFORD, VERMONT.

TO J. A. C.

As winds the lovely Otter Creek through
  vales of summer green,
   Ne'er pausing on its way,
   Though love its tribute pay,

So gently winds my loving thought through
  memory's changing scenes,
   To days of long ago
   When thee I first did know.

Thy heartfelt sympathy and help were to
  my fresh young soul
   What these dear Vermont hills
   Are to the little rills ;

A presence near, a faithful strength, life-
    giving and serene —
Oh, hills, be now as much
To her who feels Time's touch !

In different paths, through various ways,
    we've known the world since then.
Together now we rest
On Nature's peaceful breast.

CHILDHOOD'S DAYS.

TO M. C.

If knowledge gained in later years
  May wholly cloud from sight
The glimpse which childhood's eye hath
    caught
  Of heaven's celestial light,

Then need we not the atmosphere
  Of second childhood's days
To catch another broader glimpse
  Of heaven's immortal rays?

Ah, yes; we even need to seek,
  Through earth's illusive hour,
Immortal childhood's heavenly days
  Of sweet, revealing power;

For how can otherwise we catch
  The deeper glimpses yet
Of life eternal, glorious, pure,
  Where sun hath never set?

AN ANSWER.

TO B. P. S.

"Why don't I write a story?"
Ah, friend, if you could see
The depths of hidden heart-life
Alas! so known to me,

You'd find the truest story
Flashed out in gleams of light,
Before which all pens falter
And vanish out of sight.

And as they vanish from me
They leave the impress clear,
That only Heaven's pen could write
Such stories acted here.

94

So in His book of life,
　Revealed to all some day,
You'll find my story grand and true,
　Worked out in His own way.

WHERE? WHAT? WHENCE?

The kingdom of heaven is where?
   Oh, where?
Would that the heart which with pity o'er-
 flows,
While deigning love's burdens to share,
   Could disclose!

The kingdom of heaven is what?
   Oh, what?
Would that the Infinite Presence which
 flows
Through a life on the earth finely cut
   Might disclose!

The kingdom of heaven is whence?
   Oh, whence?

Ah ! let the wind and the breath of the rose
  Their secrets of life and of sense
      Dare disclose !
Could we then see the better whence spirit
    arose ?
  Who knows ?   Oh, who knows ?

HEROES.

The heroes on the battlefield are calm in
    death,
      Their fighting o'er ;
They feel no more the fevered breath
      Of battle's war ;
They hear at last the voice that saith
      " Fight on no more."

But oh, the heroes on the grander field of
    peace,
      Who know no rest !
Whose hearts ne'er feel the full release
      From mortal quest,
Nor breathe the air where struggles cease
      The soul to test.

For such we mourn, O purifying soul of
    life,
       For such we pray.
    Let Nature free them from the strife
       Of falsehood's way,
    And Love through every struggle rife
       Have free, full play.

A MAGDALEN'S EASTER CRY.

In the different mansions of heavenly space
  Prepared for the faithful and pure,
  (Ah me, for the faithful and pure!)
Can I dare hope to find e'en a small resting
    place
  Free from sin and all earthly allure?

Can a soul such as mine, that has wasted
    life's wealth
  On the baubles and gewgaws of time,
  (Ah me, on the baubles of time!)
Have a fitting strength left to regain needed
    health
  For the life of a heavenly clime?

For a life where the laws of the spirit, not
    sense,
Bring their perfect eternal reward,
(Ah me, their eternal reward !)
And the pleasures obtained with such fever
    intense
Can find nowhere a vibrating chord?

Oh, woe is me, woe is me, this Easter day !
No hope riseth up in my soul.
(Ah me, my poor sin-laden soul !)
I have only the dregs of my pleasure to pay,
    And such wrong, bitter thoughts of life's
    whole.

But, listen ! What's that ? What's that mes-
    sage I hear
Bearing down on my sad troubled heart?
(Ah me, on my sad troubled heart !)

"Christ is risen indeed. He is risen to
  cheer,
And His strength to the weakest impart."

O Christ, can it be that Thine own risen
  strength
Can give life, added life, to my soul,
To my sin-laden, weak, starving soul?
Yes, 'tis true. I'll believe, and rejoice now
  at length
To feel Easter's sweet joy o'er me roll.

FOR THE ANNIVERSARY OF MRS. BROWNING'S DEATH.

June 29, 1861.

" 'Tis beautiful," she faintly cried,
Then closed her weary eyes and died.

So stands plain fact on history's page,
Attested to by friend and sage.

But in our hearts the fact grows bright,
Illumined with immortal light.

For open eyes saw heaven's shores,
And life, not death, revealed its stores.

" 'Tis beautiful ! " It must be so,
If such a soul 'midst parting's woe,

103

Could with truth's perfect clearness see
The secret of life's mystery;

Could *know* that fullest life of man
Needs heaven's light to round God's plan.

O woman-soul without a peer,
We thank thee more and more each year

For this sweet proof of Beauty's power
Beyond earth's transitory hour.

It calms our hours of doubt and pain,
And beautifies earth's troubled reign,

To feel that thou art sending still
This same sweet message of God's will,

Born of fruition's grander sight,
Of perfect beauty, peace, and light.

ROBERT BROWNING.

"A peace out of pain,
Then a light, then thy breast.
O thou soul of my soul, I shall clasp thee again,
And with God be the rest!"
— *Prospice.*

Fulfilled December 12, 1889.

Oh, the blessed fruition
Of peace out of pain!
Of a light without darkness,
A clasping again!
Of a full soul reunion
In Love's endless reign!

Sing, O earth, with new joy
At this victory won!
For the faith that endured
Till the setting of sun!

For the hope that shone clear
    Through the mighty work done !
For the love that sought God
    To guide love here begun !
Sing, O earth, with new joy
    For such victory won !

TO NEPTUNE, IN BEHALF OF
S. C. G.

O Neptune, in thy vast survey
  Of all the ships that sail,
Watch lovingly the well-known way
  Of one we wait to hail.

The Cephalonia is her name —
  But why need I tell more?
Thou knowest indeed the well earned fame
  She bears from shore to shore.

But since among her company's band
  Is one who's life to me,
O Neptune, bear her in thy hand
  E'en yet more tenderly,

107

O'er gentle waves, 'neath fair blue sky,
 'Midst winds that only blow
To make the time more swiftly fly
 For hearts that hunger so.

Boston, September 4, 1886.

TO THE PANSIES GROWING ON THE GRAVE OF A. S. D.

Beautiful pansies, ye must know
  Your sacred mission here,
For how could otherwise ye grow
  So sweet and full of cheer?

Your watchful love we can't o'errate,
  As, lingering here in tears,
Fond memory brings the precious weight
  Of friendship's golden years.

Ye are the symbols, pure and sweet,
  Of heartsease and of life,
Through which our thought may dare retreat
  From pain and death so rife,

To realms of light and peace above,
    From earth's alloy set free,
Wherein abide immortal love
    And deathless ministry.

But still, while we your comfort seek,
    Our hearts will wildly yearn
To hear once more the loved one speak,
    Once more the form discern.

At Woodlawn Cemetery, May, 1886.

A BROKEN HEART.

I.

Must I always look for sorrow
  On the morrow?
Must I never have the hope
That a life of larger scope
Will before my vision ope?

II.

Ah, 'tis true there is but sorrow
  On the morrow
For the broken hearts that wait,
Bearing secretly their fate.
Yet the opening of the gate
To the blessed heaven's morrow,
When the aching, longing heart

Shall be free from pain and sorrow,
Comes before my tired eyes
With a wondrous sweet surprise.

III.

But this joy is not for me,
      Not for me.
Alas ! for my poor broken heart,
With its poisoned arrow's dart.
Without hope, alone, apart.

MY RELEASE.

I hear in the ocean's restless moan
    My soul's lament.
    Will it ever cease ?

I feel in the rumbling earthquake's groan
    Deep anguish spent.
    Shall I now know peace ?

I see in the smallest heaven's loan
    Enough for content —
    But is that release ?

        O no !
My release is but found in the pure under-
    tone,
    Coming nearer and dearer to me,

Of a great human love beyond Nature at
best,
Eternal, inspiring, and free.
Oh, that's my release.
Happy me, happy me !

THE GOD OF MUSIC.

TO E. T. G.

Out from the depths of silence
The god of music came,
To echo heavenly cadence
On earth's fair shores of fame.

Full-orbed, with heavenly glory,
He met the lords of earth.
But 'twas the old, old story,
They blind were to his worth.

So back to depths of silence
He flew on wings of light,
" To bide their time of nonsense,"
He sang when out of sight.

And as rolled on the ages,
   He ever and anon
Sent down to earth his pages
   The lords to breathe upon.

At length he felt vibrations,
   From Germany's fair clime,
Of sweetest modulations
   E'er heard in realms of time.

So forth he flew in rapture
   To that dear father-land,
To seize — ere earth could capture —
   A spirit pure and grand,

To which he could surrender
   Himself with perfect ease,
And weave the music tender,
   Of heaven's own harmonies.

He found the child Beethoven ;
On him his blessing fell.
And in his soul was woven
The sounds we know so well.

TO WILHELM GERICKE.

(On the completion of his conductorship of the Boston Symphony Orchestra.)

1884–1889.

Great poets can without the aid
    Of kindred mind
Reveal to us the secrets laid
    On them to find;
But music-kings need ministries
To sound their hidden harmonies.

For showing us the inmost heart
    Of these great kings,
And making clear with wondrous art
    Their wanderings,
We thank thee, while we tender here
A "bon voyage" to home's loved sphere.

FOR E. T. F.

I.

AFTER THE BIRTH OF HER SON, R. A. F.

May 28, 1887.

I'd rather hear my baby's coo,
    That little gurgling coo,
Than rarest song or symphony
Born out of music's mystery
    Which once did woo.

I'd rather see my baby's face,
    That lovely dimpled face,
Than all the choicest works of art,
Inspired by loving hand or heart,
    Contained in space.

I'd rather feel my baby's eyes,
    Such deep blue heavenly eyes,
Than all the world's delighted gaze,
Proclaiming with continued praise
    My power to rise.

O yes, 'tis true, my baby dear,
    My precious baby dear,
Is more than music, art, or fame,
Or anything that bears the name
    Of pleasure here.

For in this joy I find a rest,
    A soul-inspiring rest,
Beyond the wealth of fame or art,
To satisfy my woman-heart,
    Or make it blest.

And as I live in this my gift,
    My heaven-sent, blessed gift,

Thoughts such as Mary pondered o'er
Deep in her heart in days of yore
   Come to uplift,

And make the claims of motherhood,
   Dear sacred motherhood,
Become creation's mountain height,
Whereon e'er shines the beacon-light
   Of womanhood.

Chelsea, Mass.

II.

AFTER THE DEATH OF R. A. F.

February 5, 1888.

Would I could see my baby's face,
That lovely dimpled face,—

O God, how can I bear the pain
Of never seeing it again,
   My baby's face ;

Of never seeing in those eyes,
   Those deep blue heavenly eyes,
The wondrous glimpses of soul-light
Which filled my heart with strange delight
   And sweet surprise ;

Of never hearing baby's coo,
   That little gurgling coo —
O God, how can I bear the pain
Of never hearing it again,
   My baby's coo.

Alas!   "Thy will, not mine, be done."
   Not mine, but Thine, be done.
I can but breathe again this prayer,
As in the days of past despair,
   When peace was won.

TO C. H. F.

(Upon receiving a twig of green from the grave of Helen Hunt Jackson, October, 1888.)

With reverent touch and grateful heart,
Dear thoughtful friend,
I hold this precious bit of green
You kindly send
From Cheyenne's holy, lonely grave,
Where pilgrims tend.

It touches springs of tenderest life
Inspired by her,
Who, child of poetry and ease,
Did not demur
From sacrificing all to be
Wrong's arbiter.

That rare mosaic it suggests
Made by the hand
Of those who seek this favored spot
In chosen land,
Where, oft in life, she penned her soul
At Truth's command.

'Tis true, she wished no monument
To mark the place;
But must she not be satisfied
To see the space
Thus blessed and open to the heart
Of every race?

O brain of power and heart of fire,
America's pride,
No wonder that the mountain height,
Above sin's tide,
Was chosen as the resting place
With death to hide;

For such could give the needed rest
On earth denied,
Could satisfy the poet's thought,
Unsatisfied,
And symbolize the soul's true rest
When glorified.

AN ANNIVERSARY POEM.

And is time marked in heaven? Dost know,
    O spirit friend,
'Tis just a year ago to-day
Thou went so suddenly away,
And left me in my loneliness the weary
    days to spend? —
        Ah, weary days,
        Denied thy praise
And all thy many helpful ways!

And is earth known in heaven? Dost see,
    O clear-eyed soul,
The present changing life of man
Still working out the wondrous plan

Of making even broken lives add to the
    complete whole?—
        Ah, broken lives
        That death deprives
Of help like thine that heavenward strives!

And are we known in heaven? Do I, thy
    once fond care,
Still have that patient yearning love
Which longed to lift my soul above
The sweet though transitory joys of even
    earth's best fare?—
        Ah, earth's best fare
        Cannot compare
With thy ideal of me laid bare!

A COMFORT.

TO S. R. H.

I have sowed in tears,—
Shall I reap in joy?
Shall my human heart be satisfied,
And sorrow and pain be justified?
Shall full fruition free my soul
From limitation's sad control,
And all my faculties of mind
Their perfect rest and freedom find?

"They that sow in tears
Shall reap in joy,"
Sang a poet-heart in the long ago,
'Midst depths of sorrow, pain, and woe;
And what to him was truth and life
Has shone through all the ages' strife,
To be at last our beacon-light
Of comfort in the darkest night.

AN ANNIVERSARY.

The autumn tints of these loved hills
  Outlined against the sky,
Are dearer far to me this year
  Than in the years gone by :

For they are colors Nature wears
  To celebrate the time
When her pet child changed life on earth
  For that of heavenly clime.

She thus rejoices, while our hearts
  Wear not their flowers of joy.
Alas ! could she but give us back
  Our gifted artist boy !

But then she sees that it was best
- That he, like her, should know
Death, and the Resurrection too,
The fullest life to show. ·

A THANK-OFFERING.

TO MISS ELIZABETH P. PEABODY.

Thou priestess of pure childhood's heart,
  Wherein God's spirit lies,
Thou willing priestess of the art
  Of true self-sacrifice,

Ere thy rare spirit takes its flight
  To realms beyond our praise,
Where childhood's pure eternal light
  Shines through the blessed days,

We thank thee for thy legacy
  Of thought wrought out in deed, .

131

By which love's sweet supremacy
Becomes man's potent need.

*   *   *   *   *

Our nation must thy secret share,
Ere it can fully rise
To heights of truth and insight where
True wisdom's glory lies.

AT LIFE'S SETTING.

Put your arms around me.
    There — like that.
I want a little petting
    At life's setting.
For 'tis harder to be brave
When feeble age comes creeping,
    And finds me weeping
        (Dear ones gone),
Or brings before my tired eyes
Sweet visions of my youth's fair prize
    (There is a pain in sacrifice),
Denied me then and ever.
Left me alone ?   No, never.
For in God's love I nestled,
While with deep thought I wrestled,

Till all my busy life at length
Was spent in giving others strength,
In making others' homes more bright,
In making others' burdens light.

But now, alone and weary,
I am hungry
For a human love's sweet petting
At life's setting.
Keep your arms around me,
Kiss my fevered brow,
Whisper that you love me —
I can bear it now.

Oh, how this does rest me
Now my work is done !
I've all my life loved others,
Now I want love, dear one.

Just a little petting
At life's setting ;
For I'm old, alone, and tired,
And my long life's work is done.

GRANDMA WAITING.

A TRUE EXPERIENCE.

" Still waiting, dear good grandma, for the
blessed angel Death ? "

"Yes waiting, only waiting to be borne
across the sea,
To the home my soul's been building all
these years of mystery,
Through ninety years and over now of deep
and wondrous change,
Wherein I've known the heights and depths
of human feeling's range,
And tried to solve the problems old of
human life so strange.

*   *   *   *   *   *

136

You want to know my history, because I
   am so good?
Ah, child, no human life can here be fully
   understood.
You call me good, and what is more, a
   'true and blessed saint.'
(There is illusion sweet indeed in what you
   child-souls paint
Before you know too much of life and feel
   its evil taint.)
You even picture beauties of my home
   across the sea
Which I never dared to hope for e'en on
   heights of ecstasy.
You see me sitting helpless here, blind
   now for many years,
Apparently so full of peace, so free from
   doubts and fears,—
Though never free from Memory's thought
   which often brings the tears,—

And you wonder where's the passion and
    the energy of youth,
The power that even dared to sway to evil
    ways forsooth.
Ah, you but see the blessed fruit of what
    God planted sure,
When in my years of sorrow He was whis-
    pering, ' Endure.'
You cannot see the dreadful scars which
    naught on earth can cure.
You cannot see the passion wild, when,
    'neath the coffin lid,
Among the flowers, my children three, my
    precious all, were hid.

Nor can you see my conflict sore, when I
    went almost mad
Before the dying form of him who had
    loved me from a lad,

A loving husband, kind and true, as ever
    woman had.
But still, before my dear one died, more
    children came to me :
Two lovely boys, who seemed at last a
    recompense to be.
For sometimes it does seem as if God sends
    a special gift,
To be a special help and strength, the sel-
    fish clouds to lift,
Or — what, perhaps, we need as much— the
    wheat from chaff to sift.
Through all my lonely, widowed life I lived
    in their sweet ways,
And found no sacrifice too great in work
    for future days.
At length they were my crowning joy. I'd
    come again to know
The blessings of a married life — the hap-
    piest here below —

And been as good for duties here, as fit for
　　heaven's reign ?
Was this the way, the only way, eternal life
　　to gain ?

It cannot be much longer.　I shall soon
　　have crossed the sea,
To the home my soul's been building all
　　these years of mystery.
I've had my share of sorrow, but I've done
　　the best I could.
God knows I've tried through all to grow
　　more patient, wise, and good ;
To get at least this out of life, as every
　　mortal should.
But, though I've had his comfort, and still
　　hear his sweet ' Endure,'
I feel the bitter heartache which no time
　　or sense can cure.

My friends have all been laid away, my
 work long since was o'er,
And now I'm only waiting for Death's
 landing on the shore.
I hope 'twill be at sunset when he knocks
 at my soul's door ;
For, somehow, it much easier seems to go
 the unknown way
Attended by the beauty of the sun's last
 glorious ray.
But as I calmly wait and think, it does
 seem rather queer
That what you 'blessed angel' call has
 seemed my chief curse here.
Alas ! how much we suffer before God's
 ways appear."

DOES IT PAY?

Does it pay — all this burden and worry,
  All the learning acquired with pain,
All the planning and nervous wild action,
  The restlessness following gain,
      Does it pay?

To be free from this burden and worry,
  To have knowledge without fear and pain,
To be peaceful, far-seeing, sweet tempered,
  And calm in the presence of gain,
We must know the pure secret of Nature,
  Like her be obedient to law,   ·
And work in the light of the promise
  Of blessed results Christ foresaw.
      Then each day,
      And alway,
      Life will pay.

144

AUXILIUM AB ALTO.

The poet young e'er finds a tongue
  To tell the joys of love.
The poet bold e'en dares behold
  The mystery above.

The poet brave e'er loves to rave
  Of wars and victories gained.
The poet sweet e'en dares repeat
  The angels' songs unfeigned.

And to each one we say, " Well done,
  Go on and do thy best."
Though still we feel each doth but seal •
  A part of life's bequest.

145

But yet we cry, " O goddess high,
    Must thou thy wealth so share?
America feign would have the reign
    Of *one* thy gift to bear.

She needs such one to help her shun
    The dangerous shoals of thought,
Which in this age of clown and sage
    Her progress gained hath wrought.

She needs such one to help her shun
    The deeper shoals of wrong,
Which in these days of doubt's fond lays
    Tempt e'en her favored strong.

Oh, send such one to say, ' Well done,'
    And tell in truth God's plan,
While he declares as well as shares
    The fullest life of man."

LIMITATIONS.

" Would that my acts could equal the noble
 acts I've told.
Would that I could but master myself as
 visions bold ! "

So cried a famous artist, in agony of soul,
As waves of great temptation before him
 high did roll.

" Oh, would that I could body the thoughts
 that govern me.
Oh, would that I could picture the visions
 I foresee ! "

So cried a saintly woman, in ecstasy of
 pain,
As waves of sad depression rolled on her
 soul to gain.

THE MUSE OF HISTORY.

Clio, with her flickering light
   And book of valued lore,
Comes down the ages, dark and bright,
   Our interest to implore.

She walks with glad majestic mien,
   Proud of her knowledge gained;
Though mourning oft at having seen
   Man's life so dulled and pained.

Her face with lines of care is wrought,
   From searching mystery's cause,
And dealing with the hidden thought
   Of nature's subtle laws.

Yet still she blushes with new life
   At sight of actions fine,
And pales with anguish at the strife
   Of evil's dread design.

She stops to sing her grandest lays
   When, in creation's heat,
She sees evolved a higher phase
   Of life's fruition sweet.

'Twas thus in days of Genesis,
   When man came forth supreme.
'Twas thus in days of Nemesis,
   When Love did dare redeem.

And thus 'twill be in future days,
   When out from spirit laws,
Shall be brought forth for lasting praise
   The ever great First Cause.

Oh, gladly know this wondrous muse
Who walks the aisles of Time,
And not so thoughtlessly refuse
Her book of lore sublime ;

· For in it is the precious force
Of spirit-life divine,
Which even through a winding course
Leads in to Wisdom's shrine.

AN IMPROMPTU.

(Written for G. H. T., on the death of W. S. T., March, 1889.)

As brothers here we've shared the smiles,
The tears of boyhood's hour,
And felt the sweet companionship
Of manhood's love and power.

But now the tie is snapped.   He's fled
Beyond the mortal sight.
The grave with all its mystery
Asserts Death's power to blight.

Alas! Death seems the cruel thing
In this bright world of ours.
The bravest soul shrinks from its hold
Though loving faith empowers.

But, hark! Is 't not his voice I hear,
   With comfort as of yore?
"Dear brother, Death is but more Life,
   The grave is heaven's door."

TO MRS. PARTINGTON.

July 12, 1886.

Another birthday here ?
It hardly seems a year
Since I these words did hear,—
When three score years and one did crown
    thee,—
" Not till I am an octagon,
Or, worse still, a centurion,
Shall I be old, with factories gone
All idiomatic and forlorn."

But thou art still a "membrane" dear
Of what we call society's cheer ;
" Ordained beforehand, in advance."
('Twas "foreordained," that does enhance,)

153

To hurl not "epitaphs" which sting,
But a new "Erie's" dawn to bring,
Of "fluid" thoughts which counteract
The "bigamies" of fate and fact.

Alas ! thy crutch of many years
Still hints "romantic" pains and fears ;
A "Widow Cruise's oil jug" say,
To keep "plumbago" still at bay !

Its helpful mission has a share
In "Lines of Pleasant Places" rare.
And, by the way, not crutch alone
Finds in that book its value shown.

There in the depths of friendship's mines
Are seen thy tenderest, purest lines ;
Impromptus born at love's command
To deck occasion's wise demand.

One finds no " Sarah's desert " there,
No " reprehensible " despair ;
But teeming thoughts on Mounds and Press
Poured out in pure unselfishness.

This brings to mind thy *Knitting-Work*,
Wherein that "plaguey Ike" does lurk,
And other books with humor rife,
Done in the priming of thy life.

"Contusion of ideas." O no ;
What " Angular Saxon " would say so ?
" Congestive thoughts then so inane
They'd decompose the soundest brain."

Yes, there it is, thy humor still,
Not seventy years and two can kill.
'Tis free from all "harmonious" lore,
A "wholesome" not a "ringtail" store.

LINES

SENT TO THE DINNER GIVEN IN HONOR OF WALT
WHITMAN'S SEVENTIETH BIRTHDAY, AT CAM-
DEN, N.J., MAY 31, 1889, AT 5 O'CLOCK P.M.

" Splendor of ended day floating and filling
    me,"*
Comes to my mind as I think of the hour
When our poet and friend will be lovingly
    drinking
The mystical cup of the seventy years'
    power.

Were I the man-of-war bird he has pictured
Nothing could keep me from flying that
    way.

*"Song at Sunset."— *W. W.*

156

But, though absent in body, there's nothing
 can hinder
My tasting the joys of that festive birth-
 day ;

For on the swift wings of the ending day's.
 splendor
My soul will glide in to drink deep the
 cup's wealth.
Who knows but the poet's keen sense of
 pure friendship
Will feel, 'midst the joy, what I drink to
 his health ? —
   Splendor of ended day
   Be but the door
   Opening the endless way
   Life evermore.

Upon leaving the San Sisto Madonn
e "

They say in the heavenly mansions,
That Beauty will show us her best;
Her rarest Madonnas and Cherubs,
And Angels we've dreamed of as fleet.
And while they are telling the story
(I wonder if she will forget
To come for our lonely Madonna
The one that her Raphael set

On the clouds to await her fair comin'
With Cherubs to open the way,
And saints that eternally worship
The light of the heavenly day.
(If true be thy mission, San Sisto
O queen of the art of this world,
May I in that heavenly mansion
Again see thy beauty unfurled.

Dresden. 1894.   E. P. G.

SONNETS.

On the Heights.

- To my mother -

On highest point of Washington's grand pe[ak]
I humbly stood. A perfect day and nigh[t]
Had filled my being with that pure deli[ght]
Felt by the saints when holy angels spe[ak]

"O Father," cried I. "Thee alone I seek
To make me worthy of this glorious h[eight]
O may my soul's horizon be as bright
As broad, free from the petty and the wea[k]

So on Truth's highest rock we sometimes s[tand]
In ecstasy. The beauteous peaks of lo[ve]
Reveal the glories of a broader life,
A fuller joy, unknown to lower land.
'Tis then our quickened prayers find light ab[ove]
To flower in noble acts upon a world of strife.

1892.   E. P. B.

THE KNOWN GOD.

(Suggested by Arlo Bates' sonnet, "The Unknown God," published in the BOSTON COURIER *of August 21, 1887.)*

If Paul in Athens' street left nothing more
Than what he found when deep in sacred
thought,
He stood and marvelled o'er what had
been wrought,—
The *To the Unknown God* of heathen
lore,—   .
Then were he only one on thought's wide
shore
To lose his name in others.   But, heaven-
taught,

161

Undaunted, and in words experienced-
   fraught,
Declared he God as known forevermore.

Paul's words, made deep and strong by
   martyred life,
Are more than vision deified.   They are
Love's balm to permeate true mental strife,
   And bring to sin-sick weary souls a star
Of hope born of temptation's struggles rife.
   To the Known God.   Through Paul we
   dare thus far.

August, 1887.

TO PHILLIPS BROOKS.

O type of manhood, strong, serene, and
    chaste,
Attuned to law of man as well as God,
We hail thee as a guide, who, having
    trod
With Christ the spirit-fields, in eager haste
Makes glad return to give us blessed taste
    Of fruit there found.   Through thee our
    feet are shod
    With gospel-peace, while thy imperial
    rod
Becomes our need in times of drought or
    waste.

How can we thank thee for thy helpful
    cheer,

O master-spirit of the priests of earth?
By daily doing penance without fear,
    Or resting satisfied in deeds of worth?
O no!   'Tis when we breathe love's at-
    mosphere,
And live like thee the life of heavenly
    birth.

Boston, 1890.

AT THE "PORTER MANSE."

[That part of the Porter Manse containing the room referred to was built early in the last half of the seventeenth century. It was the house which Wenham (the first distinct township set off — in 1639 — from Salem) gave to the second pastor of its church, Rev. Antipas Newman, who married, while living there, Governor Winthrop's daughter. It was bought by John Porter in 1703, and has remained in his family name without alienation to this day.]

Before a smouldering fire at twilight hour
I muse alone. The ancient room, low-
    beamed,
Holds for my ear thoughts voiced by
    forms that teemed
Two hundred years ago with life and power.
I breathe the essence of sweet joys that
    flower

In light of home; while life that only
  seemed
On history's page becomes the real, re-
  deemed
From all the chaff that time fails not to
  shower.

Ah, such old places, holding through the
  years
Continuous life of man's activity,
Reveal a wealth beyond that which appears
  In modern homes built e'er so lovingly.
Imbued so long with human hopes and
  fears,
  Have they not claim to personality?

OUR LADY OF THE MANSE.

Of all those born into the name to share
  The charming freedom of the Porter
  Manse,
None were more worthy of inheritance
Than she who now presides as lady there.
Her gracious calm makes hospitality wear
  A beauteous crown of peace. Kind tol-
  erance
And wide-embracing sympathy enhance
Her power to please and lighten daily care.

'Tis only such rare souls who pierce the
  truth
Of home-life secrets, and through tact
  and grace,

Make growing years reflect the joys of
  youth.
  They lose not hope, though sorrow leave
  a trace
In all their joy. Such cannot fail, forsooth,
  Of making home a loved abiding place.

TO B. P. SHILLABER.

July 12, 1888.

When lingering Day at last recedes from
    sight,
And Night comes slowly forth to fill her
    place,
Preceded by a twilight-hour's loved face
Reflecting glorious rays of sunset light,
'Tis then my thoughts go wandering with
    delight
Through oft-frequented avenues of space
To those dear souls — the dearest of the
    race —
Who've dwelt with me on friendship's purest
    height.

From this old mountain-top I come to you,
  My large souled trusted friend of many
    a year,
With birthday greetings of the roseate hue
  Left by a perfect Day just lingering here.
Oh, may life's twilight hold a peace as
    true,
  And be as filled with hope of dawn's
    sweet cheer!

Mount Wachusett, Mass.

TO OUR MARY.

Sweet sister, thoughtful ever of our need,
Forgetting self, if only we be served,
How oft thy loving sympathy has nerved
Our fainting hearts to kinder, nobler deed,
Or brought to being thoughts that inter-
    cede
For others' progress.   We, all unde-
    served,
Cannot forget that life to ends thus
    curved
Made time for us to plant our own pet
    seed.

The world owes much to many a sister
    dear,

Who, banishing with tears in midnight
hour
A fond desire for larger, happier sphere,
Strives faithfully in lowly life to shower
Rich daily blessings. Such may know e'en
here
A Christ-like joy unknown to worldly
power.

Chelsea, Mass., 1887.

A BIRTHDAY REMEMBRANCE.

TO F. D. L.

September 26.

Time brings to thee from out his storehouse
 old
Another year, which graciously awaits
Thy fair soul's bidding, as it estimates
The wealth the parting year has left un-
 told.
Clothed in chameleon garments, which
 unfold
The fresh new days thine eye ne'er
 underrates,
It brings continued hope of life that
 dates
Man's finest being. Thou its secrets hold !

Are not such birthdays restful stepping
    stones,
  To aid the growing soul pick out the way
To life eternal? Not earth's bitterest moans
  Or wildest joys can man's true progress
    stay,
If, in these pauses, he but hear the tones
  Of immortality's soothing, deathless lay.

1887.

JOSEF HOFMANN.

(After hearing him play at Boston Music Hall in 1888.)

O marvellous child, a temple where in ease
Expectant Genius dwells, while lingering
  here
On earth to fit us for the heavenly sphere,
Dost feel awe-struck to know thou hast the
  keys
To new and wondrous unheard harmonies?
O favored boy, marked out to be the peer
Of those who in all ages God's voice hear,
Hushed are our souls before what thy soul
  sees!

Guard tenderly, O earth, O sky, O fates,
This precious earthly temple of Art's
  shrine!

May chilling poverty, or sin that dates
   Soul loss, ne'er hinder Genius' wise de-
      sign
To have full sway — as she anticipates —
   In working out, in time, her laws divine.

I.

John 21 : 15-18.

When fast was broken on Tiberias' shore,
The risen Lord, still anxious that his own
Should know love's secret as to him 'twas
  known,
Thrice asked of Peter, "Lovest thou me
  more
Than these?" The third time Peter's heart
  was sore.
Must even love divine have doubt's sad
  tone?
"Thou knowest, Lord, I love thee," was
  his moan.
Then, "Feed my sheep," Christ answered
  as before.

Still in these days the risen Lord bends
o'er
The shores of time, and longs for human
love ;
The love that hears his voice, awake, asleep,
And makes response as Peter did of yore.
" Lovest thou me ? "   O Christ, from heights
above,
Thou knowest that we love thee.   " Feed
my sheep."

II.

GETHSEMANE.

Matthew 26 : 36-46.

" Could ye not watch with me one hour ? "
O heart
Of Christ, still longing in the bitterest
hour
For human sympathy and love to shower
A needed strength beyond words to im-
part !
Humanity is richer for this art
Of seeing in poor finite man a power —
Before which even ministering angels
cower —
To know all truth, e'en dread Gethsemane's
smart.

Alas! the power to know will bring the
    pain.
But through the pain of wisdom's true
    insight
Is Christ's own perfect sympathy made
    plain.
Possessed of this, we see in tenderest
    light
His sorrowing heart in failing to obtain
    The longed-for love in hour of darkest
    night.

ON LAKE MEMPHREMAGOG.

By old Owl's Head on Memphremagog's
    side,
In hammock-nook 'midst scenery wild
    and bold,
The spirit of the waters, as of old,
Broods o'er my soul, its secrets to confide,
It whispers of the anguish, joy, and pride,
    The heart of man has on its bosom told ;
    And hails as conqueror Him who once
      did hold
Its heart in peace when tempest-tossed and
    tried.

Loved spirit of the waters, we too hail
    The power of Him who walked the holy
      sea

Of Galilee.   Capacity to fail
  Were harder to believe than victory.
May He who conquered wildest Nature's
      heart
His infinite power and rest to us impart!

August, 1891.

LUKE 23 : 24.

From holy depths he to the Father prayed,
  " Forgive them, for they know not what
    they do."
  His heart, pierced then with anguish
    through and through,
Cried out " 'Tis finished," as he death
    obeyed.
In bitterest wrong this marvellous soul was
    weighed
  With tenderest love and longing towards
    those who,
  Through ignorance of what they might
    be too,
Were now the slaves of evil passion's raid.

" They know not what they do."   O blessed
        sight
Into the heart of sin's great mystery.
Forgiveness here is shown in sweetest light,
    Clothed in her garment of sincerity.
Blest are those souls who reach this precious
        height ;
    They know the secret of Christ's victory.

TO THE MEMBERS OF MY HOME CLUB.*

While dwelling in sweet wisdom's fruitful
      ways,
In company with poets grand and good
Who met our human nature's every mood,
What life was ours, beyond our words to
      praise !
In seeking for the secret of the lays
Which clothed in art pure, Nature's daily
      food,
Or brought to light a Christian brotherhood,
Did we not garner thoughts for future
      days ?

* For an account of this Home Club, see the *Boston Liter-
ary World*, of July 9, 1887, and June 9, 1888; also, *Lend a
Hand*, for September, 1889.

185

'Tis one of wisdom's joys, while lingering
   here
   To plant her seeds of righteousness and
      peace,
To give a sweet companionship and cheer
   To those who seek from her their soul's
      increase.
This, friends, we've felt in our Club atmo-
   sphere.
   May its sweet memory linger till life
      cease !

Chelsea, Mass., 1888.

FOR MY LITTLE NEPHEWS
AND NIECES.

A MAMMA'S LULLABY.

Dream of loveliest beauty in thine hour of
    sleep,
  Harold, baby boy.
  Lullaby, lullaby, lullaby.
Catch the sweetest glimpses of the heavenly
    bliss,
While the holy angels bless thee with a
    kiss.
    Lullaby, lullaby.
  So shall mamma feel a breath
    Of celestial power,
  To beautify the ministry,
    Of baby's waking hour.
  Lullaby, lullaby, lullaby,
    Harold, baby boy.
    Lullaby, lullaby.

WARREN'S SONG.

How I love you, baby dear,
　　Sister Rosamond!
　　I must kiss you,
　　I must hug you,
I must be your little beau,
　　To protect you
　　Or to rescue
From the faults of friend or foe.
I must grow more wise and graceful
　　Every way,
That I may be true and helpful
　　For the day
When, as lovely fair young woman,
　　You will need my stay.
　　Darling Rosebud,

How I love you,
How I love you, sister dear !
Oh, I will be good and pure,
Striving always to endure
What will make me honest, kind,
Generous, manly, strong in mind,
  Worthy of my Rosebud.
    Darling Rosebud,
    Sweetest Rosebud,
How I love you, sister dear !

BABY MILDRED.

Darling baby Mildred, playing on the
    floor —
      I see !
Creeping here and creeping there,
Into mischief everywhere,
Mamma's little pet and care —
      I see !

Fearless baby Mildred, on her rocking
    horse —
      I see !
Never slipping from her place,
Joyous laughter keeping pace
With a motion full of grace —
      I see !

Thoughtful baby Mildred, papa's pet and
    pride —
        I know !
Lighting up the passing days
With such happy, winsome ways,
Joy of household life that pays —
        I know !

Tired baby Mildred, lovely eyes all closed—
        Sleep on !
Waking, heaven will be more near
For the angels' presence here,
Whispering secrets in her ear —
        Sleep on !   Sleep on !

ROSAMOND AND MILDRED.

Rosamond and Mildred, playing on the
     floor —
          I see!
Laughing blue eyes, dimpled face,
Laughing brown eyes, ways of grace,
Chubby hands that interlace —
          I see!

Rosamond and Mildred, trying hard to
     walk —
          I see!
Clinging now to mamma's dress,
Trembling in new happiness,
Then at last a sweet success —
          I see!

Rosamond and Mildred, born the same
    glad year —
        I know !
Cousins ; each in her own way
Growing wiser every day,
Full of promise as of play —
        I know !

Rosamond and Mildred, parting to go
    home —
        Good-bye !
Each a little picture fair,
Carrying blessing everywhere.
Grateful are we for our share —
    Good-bye ! Good-bye !

'CHILLA.

Chinchilla?   Come, 'Chilla! —
Ah, here she comes bounding,
So quickly responding,
Oh, who could but love her!
Her fur like chinchilla —
Her movements all grace —
Such a wise little face —
What kitty is like her?
Oh, who could but love her,
Our dear pretty 'Chilla!

CHILDISH FANCIES.

(A FACT.)

My little nephew, four years old,
A sweet-faced, blue-eyed boy,
Was one day playing by my side
With this and that pet toy,

When all at once he said to me,—
As, laying down my book,
I paused a while to watch with joy
His bright, expressive look,—

"If Mac and I should plant today
Some paper in the ground,
Say, would it grow to be a book
Like yours, with leaves all bound?"

197

These were the same two little boys
  Whose nurse searched far and wide
For little sister's rubber shoes ;
  " Where can they be ? " she cried.

" I know," replied Mac, eagerly,
  " We planted them last night,
To see if they would bigger grow
  To fit our feet all right."

Dear little boys !   These fancies hint
  Of future questions deep,
When evolution's grand idea
  Shall o'er their vision sweep.

God grant that when these come to them,
  As at Truth's shrine they bow,
A childlike faith and earnestness
  May fill them then as now.

WHAT LITTLE BERTRAM DID.

(A FACT)

Our little Bertram, six years old,
  Sat on his grandpa's knee,
Enjoying to the full the love
  That grandpa gave so free,

When, looking up bewitchingly,
  He said,— the little teaze,—
" Will grandpa give me just one cent
  To buy some candy, please ? "

Who could resist such loveliness ?
  This grandpa could not, sure.
So with a kiss he gave the cent —
  Ah, how such things allure !

No sooner was the cent in hand,
   Than off the fair boy ran
To buy his candy, " 'lasses kind,"
   Or little " candy-man."

Now on his way, in scanning well
   A window full of toys,
He spied a ring with big red stone,
   O'erlooked by other boys.

All thôught of candy was forgot.
   He'd buy that ring so fine
For his new sister, Rosamond —
   Oh, how his eyes did shine!

How could he stop to calculate
   The size of such a thing;
His only care was for the price —
   Would one cent buy the ring?

Ah yes, it would.   The ring was bought ;
And never girl or boy
Went tripping homeward through the
streets
With greater wealth or joy.

"DEAR LITTLE MAC."*

(A FACT.)

When nearly eight years old, dear little
Mac
Was called from out his happy home-life
here
To that blest sphere
Beyond earth's dearest power to call him
back.

" His questions wise will now sure answer
find,"
Said one who 'd loved to watch his eager
face,
In happy chase

* MacLaurin Cooke Gould, died in Maplewood, Mass., No-
vember 8, 1887.

202

Of many a thought which flitted through
   his mind.

"Yes, he knows more than we," another
   said,
"Instead of guiding him, he'll be our guide
   To where abide
The things we need most to be comforted."

While thus the older ones their comfort
   sought,
Two of the children paused in midst of
   play,
   To have their say
Concerning this great mystery Death had
   brought.

"Dear little Mac," said Miriam, with a
   sigh,

" He's gone way up to heaven where angels
　　are,
　　Way up so far
That we can't ever see him till we die."

" He's not up there," said Bertram.   " He
　　can't be.
I saw them put him in the cold dark
　　ground,
　　And I went round
And threw some flowers in for him to see."

" He isn't there," replied the four-year old,
" He's up in heaven.　My mamma told
　　me so.
　　He *is*, I know.
He isn't in the ground all dark and cold."

A moment Bertram sat absorbed in thought,
While Miriam felt the joy of victory.

Then suddenly
The lovely six-year-old this idea caught :

" I tell you what, Mac's body 's in the
    ground ;
His head, his feet, and every other part,
    But just his heart —
And that's gone up to heaven, and angels
    found."

The child thus solved the thought that
    troubled so.
And as I overheard this earnest talk,—
    Which might some shock,—
I wondered if we could more wisdom show.

As each seemed satisfied, their play went
    on.
But Bertram's thought sank deep in sister's
    mind,

And left behind
The wonder how dear Mac to heaven had
gone.

At last, when ready for their sweet "Good
Night,"
She softly said, " It can't be very dark,
Not *very* dark
For Mac, I know, 'cause God will make it
light."

Oh, lovely faith of childhood's trusting
days,   ·
Sent fresh from heaven to be our loving
guide,
When sadly tried
By doubt or sorrow's strange, mysterious
ways.

WILLARD AND FLORENCE ON MOUNT WACHUSETT.

July, 1888.

Happy little girl and boy,
    Dancing hand in hand
Over hill and valley land,
    Filled with summer joy ;

Climbing up the steep path side
    To Wachusett's top,
With that graceful skip and hop
    Born where fairies hide ;

Seeing Holyoke from the height,
    Old Monadnock clear,
While Washacum twin-lakes near
    Sparkle in sun-light ;

Tripping down the mountain-road
  Back to cottage home,
Only pausing there to roam
  Where laurel finds abode;

Jumping on the new-mown hay,
  Sitting under trees,
Feeling every mountain breeze,
  Hearing birds' sweet lay;

Lying on the mossy stone
  By the brook's cascade,
Listening 'neath the sylvan shade
  To its rippling tone;

Down at pretty Echo Lake,
  Plucking maiden-hair,
Gathering glistening "sundew" there
  For "dear mamma's sake";

Picking in the pastures near
  Berries red and blue ;
Spying where the mayflowers grew
  Earlier in the year ;

Watching for the sun to rise,
  Following sunset-cloud,
Singing low and singing loud
  While the swift day flies ;

Waiting for the " Tally-Ho,"
  With its looked-for mails,
Hearing strangers tell their tales
  As they come and go ;

Happy little girl and boy,
  Dancing hand in hand
Over hill and valley land,
  Filled with summer joy.

A LITTLE BRAZILIAN.

(A FACT.)

'Twas in Brazil last Christmas day,
  While at a family feast,
A little girl of five years old
  The merriment increased,

By crying out,—as glasses held
  The ice she ne'er had seen,—
"Oh see! what pretty little stones.
  What for? Where have they been?"

"Here, give her one," the host exclaimed,
  Pleased with her childish glee.
"'Twill show her as no words could show
  What ice is, and must be."

She grasped the "white stone" in her hand,
  All watching eagerly,
When suddenly she let it fall,
  And cried, " It's burning me."

But, anxious still to see it more,
  She asked a servant near
To hand it in a napkin wrapped —
  Then there would be no fear.

Again the ice was in her hand,
  Her plaything for the day,
When all at once she cried aloud,
  " The stone is running away."

A glass of water now was used,
  Sure that would keep it hers.
But no ! with all her loving watch
  The same result occurs.

The plaything gone, at evening hour
  She sat on uncle's knee.
" Who makes those white stones, you or
    God ? "
She asked, inquiringly.

" In Miss Brown's land [a Boston friend]
  God makes them," answered he.
" But in Brazil a factory-man
  Makes them for you and me."

A moment's pause.   Then said the child,—
  Heaven's blessing on her fall,—
" Why doesn't God get from Brazil
  A man to make them all ? "

THE LITTLE DOUBTER.

" Mamma, where is the sun to-day,
While all this rain comes down ? "
Ah, little girl
Of flaxen curl,
Who has not asked before
This question o'er and o'er ?

" Behind the clouds so thick and black
The sun is shining still,"
The mother quickly answered back,
Her child with faith to fill.

The child looked up in strange surprise,
In doubt almost a pain,
Then turned again her wistful eyes
To watch the pouring rain.

213

" I don't believe 'tis shining still,"
  She muttered to herself.
      Ah, little girl
      Of flaxen curl,
  Why doubt e'en mother's word,
  Because of feelings stirred?

" I won't believe it till I see
  The sun behind that cloud,"
She still went·on, defiantly,
  To say in accents loud.

Now, while she gazed as if to see
  The truth made known by sight,
Behold the cloud did suddenly
  Become imbued with light.

" There, there, mamma, the sun, the sun ! "
  The little doubter cried.

And, full of joy at victory won,
  She danced with childish pride.

The mother watched with tearful eyes
  Her child's transparent joy,
But dared not quench the glad surprise.
  Or victory's power destroy.

" Perhaps she'll need this proof," she sighed,
  " Of hidden things made plain,
When in the depths of life she's tried,
  And all fond hopes are slain."

While thus she mused, as mothers will,
  The little daughter fair
Rushed to her arms, all smiling still,
  And said, while nestling there.

" Behind the clouds the sun *does* shine,
E'en while the rain comes down."
Ah, little girl
Of flaxen curl,
This wisdom is indeed
For future hours of need.

OUR KITTY'S TRICK.*

I know that all the boys and girls
Would be so glad to see
Our kitty do the little trick
She often does for me.

When asked, " O kitty, where's the ball?"
She to my shoulder leaps,
And looks directly to the shelf,
Where from a box it peeps.

She will not cease to look and beg,
Until I find the place
Where she can take between her teeth
The ball with easy grace.

* These verses, true in every detail, are only preserved in remembrance of a pet cat of our family for many years.

Then quickly to the floor she jumps;
　When, dropping first the ball,
She runs behind the open door
　That leads into the hall.

She waits, with only head in sight,
　The ball to see me throw;
Then after it she scampers well
　Some forty feet or so.

She never fails to bring it back;
　Then lifts with wondrous grace
Her velvet paw to take the ball
　From out its hiding place.

This done, she nestles by my side,
　And purrs while I caress,
Unconscious of the trick she's done,
　Since three months old or less.

She thus will lie in calm repose
  So long as I am still;
But if I move to touch the ball,
  Then all her nerves will thrill,

Her eyes will shine, she'll quickly find
  Her place behind the door,
And wait again to see the ball
  Roll on the long hall floor.

Ah, kitty dear, who told you how
  To join thought, act, and sight?
Must not we think that in you dwells
  The germ of mental light,

The germ that makes you kin to us
  In kind though not degree,
But which was quickened by His touch
  For our supremacy?

A MESSAGE.

A mountain hides within itself
  This message grand and true,
Which at my bidding came to-day
  For me to give to you:

" Drink deep of Nature's sweetest life,
  While learning how to wait.
Stand strong against the tempest's strife,
  Not questioning the fate.
Then shalt thou live above the din
  Of petty things below,
Absorbing depths of life within,
  The future to o'erflow."

At the foot of Mount Holyoke.

www.ingramcontent.com/pod-product-compliance
Lightning Source LLC
Chambersburg PA
CBHW030130030726

47498CB00007B/2638